AGE
10–11
Key Stage 2

FOR THE YEAR **2005**

Mental Maths
Book 2 Levels 3–5

practice
papers

Contents	Page
Introduction	
The National Tests: A Summary	iii
Mental Maths at Key Stage 2	iv
Mental Maths Tests	
Question Pages	1
Answer Sheets	13
Answers	25
National Curriculum Levels	28
Practice Pages	
Questions	29
Answers	42

First published in 2005
exclusively for WHSmith by
Hodder Murray,
a member of the Hodder Headline Group
338 Euston Road
London NW1 3BH

Text © Hodder Murray 2005

All rights reserved. Apart from any use permitted under UK copyright law, no part of this publication may be reproduced or transmitted in any form or by any means, electronic or mechanical, including photocopying, recording, or any information storage and retrieval system, without permission in writing from the publisher or under licence from the Copyright Licensing Agency Limited. Further details of such licences (for reprographic reproduction) may be obtained from the Copyright Licensing Agency Limited, of 90 Tottenham Court Road, London W1T 4LP.

Authors: Steve Mills and Hilary Koll

Impression	5	4	3	2	1
Year			2006		2005

Printed and bound in Spain

A catalogue record for this title is available from the British Library

ISBN 0 340 88872 5

NOTE: The tests, questions and advice in this book are not reproductions of the official test materials sent to schools. The official testing process is supported by guidance and training for teachers in setting and marking tests and interpreting the results. The results achieved in the tests in this book may not be the same as are achieved in the official tests.

Introduction

The National Tests: A Summary

What are the National Tests?

Children who attend state schools in England sit National Tests (SATs) at the ages of 7, 11 and 14. Those at ages 11 and 14 are taken at the beginning of May. Those at age 7 can be carried out at any point during the year as chosen by the teacher. Children in Wales may take the same tests at 11 and 14 respectively. All children may also sit optional tests in the intervening years – many schools have chosen to adopt these tests.

The results are used by the school to assess each child's level of knowledge and progress in English and Maths at Key Stage 1 and English, Maths and Science at Key Stages 2 and 3. They also provide useful guidance for the child's next teacher.

The educational calendar for children aged 5–14 is structured as follows:

Key Stage	Year	Age by end of year	National Test
1 (KS1)	1	6	
	2	7	KEY STAGE 1
2 (KS2)	3	8	Optional Year 3
	4	9	Optional Year 4
	5	10	Optional Year 5
	6	11	KEY STAGE 2
3 (KS3)	7	12	
	8	13	
	9	14	KEY STAGE 3

Test Timetable

The Key Stage 1 National Tests have so far been carried out in May but, from the school year beginning September 2004, teachers will be allowed greater flexibility as to when they test the children and which tests or tasks they use. Key Stage 1 tests are now based on teacher assessment and can take place at any point during the year as chosen by the teacher.

Key Stage 2 tests take place in one week in May. All children sit the same test at the same time. In 2005, the tests will take place in the week of **9–13 May**. Your child's school will be able to provide you with a detailed timetable.

Key Stage 3 students will sit their tests on **3–6 May**.

Levels

National average levels have been set for children's results in the National Tests. The levels are as follows:

LEVEL	AGE 7 (KS1)	AGE 11 (KS2)	AGE 14 (KS3)
8			
7			
6			
5			
4			
3			
2			
2a			
2b			
2c			
1			

- Below expected level
- Expected level
- Above expected level
- Exceptional

Results

Your child's school will send you a report indicating his or her levels in the tests and the teacher assessment.

The school's overall test results will be included in local and national league tables, which are published in most newspapers.

What can parents do to help?

While it is never a good idea to encourage cramming, you can help your child to succeed by:

- Making sure he or she has enough food, sleep and leisure time during the test period.
- Practising important skills such as writing and reading stories, spelling and mental arithmetic.
- Telling him or her what to expect in the test, such as important symbols and key words.
- Helping him or her to be comfortable in test conditions including working within a time limit, reading questions carefully and understanding different ways of answering.

Introduction

Mental Maths at Key Stage 2

Most children at Key Stage 2 will take an orally delivered Mental Maths Test and two written tests. This book contains 12 Mental Maths Tests and practice questions for the range of topics covered.

The marks given to each child in the national Mental Maths Test are used in conjunction with the marks gained in the written tests to find out a National Curriculum Level, with a typical 11-year-old attaining Level 4.

To gain an idea of the level at which your child is working, use the table on page 28, which shows you how to convert your child's marks for each Mental Maths Test into a National Curriculum Level. Children working at the expected level or above should aim to score more than 11 marks out of 20 in each test.

Setting the tests

Do not expect your child to take the tests one after another. Taking the tests regularly over a few weeks can provide your child with sufficient practice and can help him or her to notice improvements and to track progress.

Your child will only need a pencil and rubber for each test.

Each mental test should take approximately 10–15 minutes to give. It consists of:

- A list of twenty questions to be read aloud – cut this out for ease of use.
- An answer sheet that your child should use for recording answers.

Read each question twice and allow only the time suggested for your child to answer.

Questions in the national Mental Maths Test cover a wider range than just calculation in your head. Where mental calculation is required, your child can make small jottings on the answer sheets to help him or her retain information from the question. These must NOT then be used to form the basis of written calculations: children are not allowed to 'work out' answers on paper. For example, if a question asks children to multiply 25 by 8, your child could jot down 25 and 8, but cannot then set it out as a written multiplication question to find the answer. Instead a mental method should be used, such as using a 'double, double, double' method for multiplying by 8, i.e. 25…50…100…200.

Marking the tests

Discuss the answers with your child and encourage him or her to explain the methods used to reach an answer. Any mental method that reaches the correct answer should be praised, although alternative and perhaps quicker methods can be discussed.

Keep a record of your child's scores for each test to monitor his or her progress.

"For this first set of questions you have five seconds to work out each answer and write it down."

1. What is seven multiplied by three?
2. How many months are there in two years?
3. Write the number thirteen thousand and three in figures.
4. How many grams are there in one point five kilograms?
5. What is three-tenths as a decimal?
6. What number is four less than five thousand?

"For the next set of questions you have ten seconds to work out each answer and write it down."

7. A pen costs seventy pence and a pencil case costs one pound ninety-nine pence. How much do the pen and pencil case cost altogether?
8. The temperature yesterday was two degrees Celsius. The temperature today is eight degrees colder. What is the temperature today?
9. Look at the answer sheet. In the equation, what is the value of *n*?
10. What is one-tenth of eighty-six?
11. Multiply seven by twenty-five.
12. Two numbers have a total of eighty. One number is twenty-six. What is the other number?
13. Look at the answer sheet. Circle the number that is nearest to ten metres.
14. Molly slept for nine and a half hours without waking. She went to sleep at ten p.m. What time did she wake?
15. Look at the answer sheet. What is the mean of the three test scores?

"For the next set of questions you have fifteen seconds to work out each answer and write it down."

16. Look at the answer sheet. Draw a ring around the smallest of the five numbers.
17. A regular shape has a perimeter of thirty-six centimetres. Each side is nine centimetres. What is the name of the shape?
18. I have ninety pence. My friend has four times that much. How much do we have altogether?
19. Which number is exactly half-way between two thousand and five thousand?
20. Look at the answer sheet. What is the size of angle B?

Test 4
Questions

"For this first set of questions you have five seconds to work out each answer and write it down."

1. What is four multiplied by eleven?
2. How many days are there in ten weeks?
3. Write the number ten thousand and three in figures.
4. How many millilitres are there in a quarter of a litre?
5. What is nought point seven as a fraction?
6. What is sixty multiplied by six?

"For the next set of questions you have ten seconds to work out each answer and write it down."

7. Find the difference between one hundred and ninety and three hundred and forty.
8. Add sixteen to fourteen and then multiply by three.
9. Look at the answer sheet. In the equation, what is the value of n?
10. One-third of a number is nine. What is the number?
11. Divide one thousand by one hundred.
12. The time is quarter past ten in the evening. Write this as it would be shown on a twenty-four hour digital clock.
13. Look at the answer sheet. Draw a ring around the decimal that is equivalent to ninety per cent.
14. Sam's maths lesson started at five to nine in the morning. It lasted one hour. What time did the lesson end? Write your answer in digital form.
15. Look at the answer sheet. What is the mode of these numbers?

"For the next set of questions you have fifteen seconds to work out each answer and write it down."

16. Look at the answer sheet. Draw a ring around the number nearest to one.
17. A rectangle has sides of two point six centimetres and three point four centimetres. What is its perimeter?
18. Imagine a circle. If a straight cut was made through the centre of the circle to form two identical shapes, what would these shapes be called?
19. Look at the answer sheet. Draw a ring around any of the numbers that are square numbers.
20. Look at the answer sheet. It takes forty-three minutes to get from the shopping centre to the cinema. Write what time the bus arrives at the cinema.

"For this first set of questions you have five seconds to work out each answer and write it down."

1. Write the number forty thousand and sixteen in figures.
2. What is thirty-three more than fifteen?
3. What is sixty-seven divided by ten?
4. What is two-thirds of twelve?
5. How many degrees are there in one of the angles of an equilateral triangle?
6. How many weeks are there in two years?

"For the next set of questions you have ten seconds to work out each answer and write it down."

7. Add twelve and eighteen and then divide by six.
8. What is half of seven point four?
9. Two lengths add to make one metre. One of the lengths is seventeen centimetres. What is the other length?
10. A cartoon programme lasts for twenty minutes. It starts at ten minutes to five. What time does it end?
11. A shop has fifty per cent off all prices. What is the new price of a book that was seventeen pounds?
12. On the answer sheet is part of a scale. What number is the arrow pointing to?
13. Imagine a square-based pyramid. How many of its faces are rectangles?
14. A one-litre jug is half full. How many more millilitres are needed to fill it?
15. A football team scored five goals for every two they let in. They scored fifteen goals. How many did they let in?

"For the next set of questions you have fifteen seconds to work out each answer and write it down."

16. Which number is exactly half-way between twenty-two and thirty-eight?
17. Find the total of twenty-two, thirty-three and forty-five.
18. A man was born in 1898. In what year was the man's fortieth birthday?
19. Each of the sides of a hexagon is three point two centimetres. What is its perimeter?
20. Look at the answer sheet. How many minutes does it take to get from the shopping centre to the cinema?

"For this first set of questions you have five seconds to work out each answer and write it down."

1. Two numbers have a total of one thousand. One of the numbers is six hundred and ten. What is the other number?
2. Write the number that is five squared.
3. How many five-pence pieces have the same value as three pounds?
4. How many degrees are there in half a turn?
5. Subtract seventeen from sixty.
6. The perimeter of a square is forty-four centimetres. What is the length of one of its sides?

"For the next set of questions you have ten seconds to work out each answer and write it down."

7. The time is ten to four in the afternoon. Write this time as it would be shown on a twenty-four hour digital clock.
8. Look at the number sequence on your answer sheet. What is the next number?
9. How much change from five pounds would you get if you spent exactly twelve pence?
10. Find the difference between three hundred and fifty and five hundred and ten.
11. A TV programme starts at twenty-five to seven and lasts for forty minutes. What time does the programme end?
12. On the answer sheet is part of a scale. What number is the arrow pointing to?
13. How many teams of nine people can be made from a group of fifty-four people?
14. Jane is going on a two hundred and forty kilometre journey. She travels ninety kilometres and stops. How many kilometres has she still to go?
15. Circle the fraction on the answer sheet that is equivalent to seventy-five per cent.

"For the next set of questions you have fifteen seconds to work out each answer and write it down."

16. A woman was born in 1898. In what year was the woman's sixtieth birthday?
17. Which number is exactly half-way between sixteen and thirty-two?
18. Twenty-five per cent of a number is thirteen. What is the number?
19. Circle the expression shown on the answer sheet that has an answer nearest to thirty.
20. Look at the pie chart on the answer sheet. Ninety people were asked what their favourite car was. How many people said their favourite car was a Porsche?

Test 7
Questions

"For this first set of questions you have five seconds to work out each answer and write it down."

1. What is one-quarter of twenty-eight?
2. Write the number thirty thousand and twenty-seven in figures.
3. What is eight more than twenty-seven?
4. Subtract thirty from one hundred and ten.
5. How many fifty-pence coins have the same value as seven pounds?
6. How many metres are there in five and a half kilometres?

"For the next set of questions you have ten seconds to work out each answer and write it down."

7. Add five point four and three point six.
8. What is half of two thousand and sixty?
9. A calculator costs fifteen pounds. In a sale the shop reduces all prices by ten per cent. How much does the calculator cost in the sale?
10. A TV programme lasts for fifty-five minutes. It starts at seven thirty. What time does it end?
11. A girl buys a calculator costing six pounds thirty. She pays with a ten pound note. How much change is she given?
12. On the answer sheet is part of a scale. What number is the arrow pointing to?
13. Imagine a triangular prism. How many of its faces are triangles?
14. The distance between Jo's house and the shop is one kilometre. Jo is walking from her house to the shop. She is exactly three-quarters of the way there. How many metres has she still to walk?
15. How many degrees are there in three-quarters of a turn?

"For the next set of questions you have fifteen seconds to work out each answer and write it down."

16. Which number is exactly half-way between twelve and thirty-four?
17. How many edges are there on a square-based pyramid?
18. A football team scored five goals for every two they let in. They scored twenty-five goals. How many did they let in?
19. One side of a square is ten point two centimetres. What is the perimeter of the square?
20. Circle the expression shown on the answer sheet that has an answer nearest to two hundred.

Test 8

Questions

"For this first set of questions you have five seconds to work out each answer and write it down."

1. What is eight multiplied by twenty-five?
2. Subtract sixty from three hundred and ten.
3. Write the number seventeen thousand and four in figures.
4. How many centimetres are there in one point nine metres?
5. What is seventy-five per cent as a decimal?
6. What number is four less than six thousand?

"For the next set of questions you have ten seconds to work out each answer and write it down."

7. An ice-cream costs ninety-nine pence and a lolly costs forty-five pence. How much do they cost altogether?
8. The temperature yesterday was minus three degrees Celsius. The temperature today is two degrees colder. What is the temperature today?
9. Look at the answer sheet. In the equation, what is the value of x?
10. Multiply five by nine and add six.
11. Two numbers have a difference of twelve. The higher number is sixty. What is the lower number?
12. What is one-third of twelve point nine?
13. Look at the answer sheet. Circle the number that is nearest to four kilograms.
14. Daniel slept for nine and a quarter hours without waking. He went to sleep at ten p.m. What time did he wake?
15. Look at the answer sheet. What is the median of the numbers?

"For the next set of questions you have fifteen seconds to work out each answer and write it down."

16. Look at the answer sheet. Draw a ring around the smallest of the five numbers.
17. A regular shape has a perimeter of seventy-two centimetres. Each side is nine centimetres. What is the name of the shape?
18. I have fifty pence. My friend has six times that much. How much do we have altogether?
19. Which number is exactly half-way between two thousand nine hundred and three thousand?
20. Look at the answer sheet. What is the size of angle P?

Test 9
Questions

"For this first set of questions you have five seconds to work out each answer and write it down."

1. Write the number that is ten squared.
2. Subtract forty-five from eighty.
3. Two numbers have a total of two hundred. One of the numbers is twenty-five. What is the other number?
4. How many fifty-pence pieces have the same value as twelve pounds?
5. The time is quarter past eight in the evening. Write this time as it would be shown on a twenty-four hour digital clock.
6. The perimeter of a regular hexagon is thirty centimetres. What is the length of one of its sides?

"For the next set of questions you have ten seconds to work out each answer and write it down."

7. Find the difference between one hundred and ninety-two and two hundred and eight.
8. Look at the number sequence on the answer sheet. What is the next number?
9. How much change from ten pounds would you get if you spent exactly six pounds and ninety-five pence?
10. If I add nineteen to a number I get thirty-two. What is the number?
11. A TV programme lasts for fifty minutes. It finishes at ten past four. What time does the programme start?
12. Look at the answer sheet. What is the area of the rectangle?
13. How many teams of seven can be made from a group of sixty-three people?
14. Which number is exactly half-way between one point six and one point seven?
15. Circle the decimal on the answer sheet that is equivalent to ten per cent.

"For the next set of questions you have fifteen seconds to work out each answer and write it down."

16. Seventy-five per cent of a number is thirty-three. What is the number?
17. A square has an area of four centimetres squared. What is the length of one of its sides?
18. A woman has her twenty-second birthday in the year two thousand and one. In what year was the woman born?
19. Look at the answer sheet. Circle two fractions that are equivalent to one-fifth.
20. Look at the pie chart on the answer sheet. Thirty people were asked what their favourite day of the week was. How many people said their favourite day was Saturday?

Test 10
Questions

"For this first set of questions you have five seconds to work out each answer and write it down."

1. What is the product of nine and four?
2. How many days are there in five weeks?
3. Write the number ten thousand and twelve in figures.
4. Reduce nine thousand by one.
5. How many millilitres are there in one point two five litres?
6. Write eight-tenths as a fraction in its simplest form.

"For the next set of questions you have ten seconds to work out each answer and write it down."

7. A tin of beans costs forty-five pence and a loaf of bread costs sixty-eight pence. How much do the beans and bread cost altogether?
8. The temperature yesterday was minus four degrees Celsius. The temperature today is three degrees warmer. What is the temperature today?
9. What is one-quarter of five point six?
10. Look at the answer sheet. In the equation, what is the value of q?
11. Which number is exactly half-way between four and fourteen?
12. The time is twenty-five to five in the afternoon. Write it as it would be shown on a twenty-four hour digital clock.
13. Look at the answer sheet. Circle the largest of the five numbers.
14. Lucy slept for ten and a half hours without waking. She went to sleep at nine p.m. What time did she wake?
15. Look at the answer sheet. What is the modal value of the set of numbers?

"For the next set of questions you have fifteen seconds to work out each answer and write it down."

16. There are five times as many children as adults at a funfair. There are exactly six hundred people at the fair. How many are children?
17. A regular shape has a perimeter of six point four centimetres. Each side is one point six centimetres. What is the name of the shape?
18. I have fifty-two pence. My friend has four times that much. How much do we have altogether?
19. A car park costs fifty pence. Twenty-one cars visit the car park. How much money do they pay in total?
20. Look at the answer sheet. What is the size of angle R?

Test 11

Questions

"For this first set of questions you have five seconds to work out each answer and write it down."

1. What is twice fifty-six?
2. Write the number thirteen thousand and five in figures.
3. How many sides do eight pentagons have in total?
4. What is seventeen more than ninety?
5. What is four point six multiplied by ten?
6. One-tenth of the children in a class are boys. What percentage are boys?

"For the next set of questions you have ten seconds to work out each answer and write it down."

7. How many seconds are there in one and a quarter minutes?
8. One-quarter of a number is seven. What is the number?
9. What is half of five point two?
10. A snail crawls eleven centimetres. How much further does it have to crawl to reach one metre?
11. Add four and twenty-nine and then divide by three.
12. On the answer sheet is part of a scale. What number is the arrow pointing to?
13. A shop has a sale. All items are twenty-five per cent of their original prices. A video costs two pounds in the sale. What was its original price?
14. Dean walks eight miles every day. How far does he walk in a week?
15. What is the probability that the day after March 6th will be March 12th?

"For the next set of questions you have fifteen seconds to work out each answer and write it down."

16. Look at the answer sheet. Draw a ring around the number that is nearest to three.
17. Forty per cent of a number is twenty. What is the number?
18. Which year is forty-one years before the year two thousand and two?
19. Look at the answer sheet. What is the size of angle A?
20. Which of the expressions on the answer sheet has an answer nearest to forty?

Test 12

Questions

"For this first set of questions you have five seconds to work out each answer and write it down."

1. What is sixty divided by ten?
2. Two numbers have a total of one thousand. One of the numbers is four hundred and fifty. What is the other number?
3. The time is half past three in the afternoon. Write this time as it would be shown on a twenty-four hour digital clock.
4. How many ten-pence pieces have the same value as five pounds?
5. How many weeks are there in four years?
6. What is the total number of degrees of the angles inside a rectangle?

"For the next set of questions you have ten seconds to work out each answer and write it down."

7. Add thirteen and twenty-two and then divide by seven.
8. Look at the number sequence on the answer sheet. What is the next number?
9. Two lengths add to make one metre. One of the lengths is twenty-six centimetres. What is the other length?
10. Find the difference between one hundred and sixty and three hundred and ten.
11. A film lasts for one hour and twenty minutes. It starts at ten minutes to five. What time does it end?
12. On the answer sheet is part of a scale. What number is the arrow pointing to?
13. How much change from two pounds would you get if you spent exactly one pound thirty-five pence?
14. Double three point six.
15. Imagine a hexagonal prism. How many faces does it have?

"For the next set of questions you have fifteen seconds to work out each answer and write it down."

16. Add twenty-one, forty-eight and twelve.
17. Which number is exactly half-way between fourteen and forty?
18. A man was born in 1942. How old was he on his birthday in the year two thousand?
19. Each of the sides of a hexagon is two point five centimetres. What is its perimeter?
20. Look at the answer sheet. How many minutes does it take to get from the shopping centre to the cinema?

Test 1
Answer Sheet

5-second questions

1	72
2	12,005 ✗
3	70
4	2700 grams
5	3002 ✗
6	0.9

6

10-second questions

7	32, 33
8	−3 °C
9	9	x − 2.4 = 6.6
10	07:10
11	3.2	12.8
12	8.2	6.8
13	⓪.45 0.5 0.25 3.4 ⓪.8
14	6:30 am
15	5	1 3 5 7 7

⁶·⁶
²·⁴
⁹·⁰

9

15-second questions

16	121 22 ④32 ①28 190
17	Hexagon
18	£1.50
19	5600
20	G = 150 °

5

TOTAL

20

13

Test 2
Answer Sheet

5-second questions

1	77
2	250 grams
3	180
4	0.9
5	5
6	10

6

10-second questions

7	6.2	
8	720	
9	£4.35	65p, £5
10	2/5	
11	£24	£20
12	1	(pentagon)
13	11	45p, £5
14	250 ml	
15	£10	3:1, 40 children

9

15-second questions

16	12.8	3.2 cm
17	9.2	11.1
18	42	108
19	1991	2004
20	17	⑰ 34 99 8½ 49 55½

5

TOTAL

20

Test 3
Answer Sheet

5-second questions

1	
2	
3	

4	grams
5	
6	

6

10-second questions

7	£
8	°C
9	$n - 42 = 58$
10	86
11	

12	26, …
13	9.45 m 940 cm 9.5 m 955 cm 94 cm
14	
15	$\frac{2}{10}$ $\frac{5}{10}$ $\frac{2}{10}$

9

15-second questions

16	7.779 8.001 7.81 7.8 8.01
17	
18	£

19	
20	B = °

5

TOTAL

20

15

Test 4
Answer Sheet

5-second questions

1	
2	
3	

4	ml
5	
6	

10-second questions

7	190, 340
8	
9	$n - 28 = 42$
10	
11	

12	
13	0.9 9.0 9.1 0.09 90.0
14	
15	5 6 4 5 3 8

15-second questions

16	0.7 1.1 1.09 1.11 0.8
17	centimetres
18	

| 19 | 49   72   144   101   51   4 |
| 20 | bus station 12:52 / shopping centre 12:56 / swimming pool 13:11 / cinema .... |

6

9

5

TOTAL

20

Test 5
Answer Sheet

5-second questions

1		4	
2		5	°
3		6	weeks

6

10-second questions

7	
8	
9	centimetres
10	
11	£

12	
13	
14	ml
15	5 : 2 / 15 goals

9

15-second questions

16	22, 38
17	22, 33, 45
18	1898

| 19 | 3.2 cm |
| 20 | bus station 15:42 / shopping centre 15:51 / swimming pool 16:16 / cinema 16:18 |

5

TOTAL

20

Test 6
Answer Sheet

5-second questions

1	
2	
3	
4	°
5	
6	cm

10-second questions

7	
8	25, 18, 11, 4, …
9	£
10	
11	

12 0.7 0.8

13	
14	km
15	3/4 1/7 7/10 1/75

15-second questions

16	1898
17	16, 32
18	

19 3.2 × 1.7   32 × 1.7
    0.32 × 17   0.32 × 1.7

20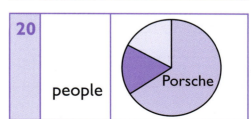
people   Porsche

/6
/9
/5
TOTAL /20

18

Test 7
Answer Sheet

5-second questions

1	
2	
3	
4	
5	
6	metres

10-second questions

7	
8	
9	£	£15
10	
11	£	£6.30
12		300 — 400
13	
14	metres
15	°

15-second questions

16		12, 34
17		edges
18		5:2 / 25 goals
19		10.2 cm
20	10.5 ÷ 20.3 105 ÷ 20.3 / 20.3 ÷ 1.05 203 ÷ 1.05

6

9

5

TOTAL

20

19

Test 8
Answer Sheet

5-second questions

1	
2	
3	

4	cm
5	
6	

10-second questions

7	£
8	°C
9	$x - 21 = 75$
10	
11	60

12	12.9
13	4.4 kg 410 g 4.5 kg 490 g 4300 g
14	
15	3 5 7 7 8

15-second questions

16	0.74 0.06 0.9 0.51 0.2
17	
18	£

| 19 | 2900, 3000 |
| 20 | P = ° |

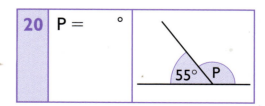

20

Test 9
Answer Sheet

5-second questions

1	
2	
3	
4	
5	
6	cm

/6

10-second questions

7	192, 208
8	100, 89, 78, 67, …
9	£
10	
11	

12	cm²	4.8 cm / 10 cm
13	
14	1.6, 1.7
15	11.0 0.1 10.0 0.01 1.0

/9

15-second questions

16	
17	□ Area = 4 cm²
18	2001

| 19 | 3/15 5/25 5/30 8/50 10/5 |
| 20 | people / Saturday |

/5

TOTAL /20

21

Test 10
Answer Sheet

5-second questions

1	
2	days
3	
4	
5	ml
6	

10-second questions

7	£
8	°C
9	5.6
10	29 + q = 63
11	4, 14
12	
13	6.45 0.5489 0.699 6.4 6.5
14	
15	4 6 2 2 3 5 2

15-second questions

16	600
17	6.4 cm
18	£
19	£ ... 50p, 21
20	R = °

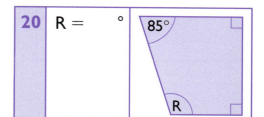

Test 11
Answer Sheet

5-second questions

1.
2.
3.
4.
5.
6. _____ %

/6

10-second questions

7. _____ seconds
8.
9.
10. _____ centimetres
11.
12. [400 ↓600 scale]
13. £
14. _____ miles
15.

/9

15-second questions

16. 3.0999   3.4   4.16   3.8   3.44
17.
18.
19. A = _____ °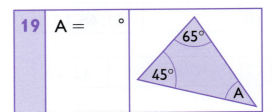
20. 8.2 × 5.5   6.1 × 8.8
    2.9 × 5.2   5.9 × 4.9

/5

TOTAL /20

23

Test 12
Answer Sheet

5-second questions

1		4	
2		5	weeks
3		6	°

10-second questions

7	
8	1, 2, 4, 8, 16, …
9	cm
10	160, 310
11	

12	0.9 ↓ 1
13	
14	
15	

15-second questions

16	21, 48, 12
17	14, 40
18	1942

| 19 | cm |
| 20 | bus station 13:42
shopping centre 13:49
swimming pool 14:08
cinema 14:12 |

TOTAL 20

24

Test 1
Questions

"For this first set of questions you have five seconds to work out each answer and write it down."

1. What is the product of nine and eight?
2. Write the number twelve thousand and five in figures.
3. Subtract forty from one hundred and ten.
4. How many grams are there in two point seven kilograms?
5. Decrease three thousand by two.
6. What is ninety per cent as a decimal?

"For the next set of questions you have ten seconds to work out each answer and write it down."

7. A number lies between thirty and forty. When it is divided by ten there is a remainder of three. What is the number?
8. The temperature yesterday was minus seven degrees Celsius. The temperature today is four degrees warmer. What is the temperature today?
9. Look at the answer sheet. In the equation, what is the value of x?
10. What time is exactly forty minutes after half past six in the morning? Give your answer in digital form.
11. What is one-quarter of twelve point eight?
12. Two numbers have a difference of one point four. One number is six point eight. What could the other number be?
13. Look at the answer sheet. Circle the number that is nearest to two-thirds.
14. Sandeep slept for nine and a quarter hours without waking. He went to sleep at nine fifteen p.m. What time did he wake?
15. Look at the answer sheet. What is the median of the numbers?

"For the next set of questions you have fifteen seconds to work out each answer and write it down."

16. Look at the answer sheet. Draw a ring around the number that is a multiple of nine.
17. A regular shape has a perimeter of forty-two centimetres. Each side is seven centimetres. What is the name of the shape?
18. I have thirty pence. My friend has five times that much. How much do we have altogether?
19. Which number is exactly half-way between five thousand three hundred and five thousand nine hundred?
20. Look at the answer sheet. What is the size of angle G?

Test 2
Questions

"For this first set of questions you have five seconds to work out each answer and write it down."

1 Add thirty-two and forty-five.
2 How many grams are there in one-quarter of a kilogram?
3 Multiply eighteen by ten.
4 Write the decimal that is equivalent to nine-tenths.
5 Divide forty-five by nine.
6 How many twenty-pence pieces have the same value as two pounds?

"For the next set of questions you have ten seconds to work out each answer and write it down."

7 Add three point six and two point six.
8 Double three hundred and sixty.
9 A girl buys a magazine, which costs sixty-five pence. She pays with a five pound note. How much change is she given?
10 A bag contains three red balls and two yellow balls. The probability of picking a red ball is three-fifths. What is the probability of picking a yellow ball?
11 A coat costs twenty pounds. In a sale the shop reduces all prices by twenty per cent. How much does the coat cost in the sale?
12 Look at the answer sheet. How many lines of reflective symmetry does the regular pentagon have?
13 A packet of crisps costs forty-five pence. How many packets can be bought for five pounds?
14 A carton of orange juice holds 1 litre. How many millilitres of juice are there when the carton is one-quarter full?
15 In a class there are three boys to every girl. How many girls are there if there are 40 children altogether in the class?

"For the next set of questions you have fifteen seconds to work out each answer and write it down."

16 One side of a square is three point two centimetres. What is the perimeter of the square?
17 Two numbers have a difference of one point nine. The higher number is eleven point one. What is the lower number?
18 There are three times as many children as adults at a funfair. There are exactly one hundred and eight people at the fair. How many are adults?
19 Which year was thirteen years before the year two thousand and four?
20 Which number on the answer sheet is an approximate answer to the question 'What is seventeen per cent of ninety-nine?'

Answers
Mental Maths Tests

Test 1

1. 72
2. 12 005
3. 70
4. 2700 g
5. 2998
6. 0.9 or 0.90
7. 33
8. −3°C
9. 9 or 9.0
10. 7:10
11. 3.2
12. 8.2 or 5.4
13. 0.8
14. 6.30 a.m.
15. 5
16. 432
17. hexagon
18. £1.80
19. 5600
20. 150°

Notes:
- The median value is the number in the middle when the set is arranged in order.
- A regular shape has equal sides and equal angles.
- To find a number half-way between two numbers, add them and divide by two.

Test 2

1. 77
2. 250 g
3. 180
4. 0.9 or 0.90
5. 5
6. 10
7. 6.2
8. 720
9. £4.35
10. $\frac{2}{5}$ or two-fifths
11. £16
12. 5
13. 11
14. 250 ml
15. 10
16. 12.8 cm
17. 9.2
18. 27
19. 1991
20. 17

Test 3

1. 21
2. 24
3. 13 003
4. 1500 g
5. 0.3 or 0.30
6. 4996
7. £2.69
8. −6°C
9. 100
10. 8.6
11. 175
12. 54
13. 955 cm
14. 7.30 a.m.
15. $\frac{3}{10}$
16. 7.779
17. square
18. £4.50
19. 3500
20. 120°

Notes:
- The mean value can be found by adding the scores and dividing by the number of scores, in this case 3.
- The angles inside a four-sided shape (a quadrilateral) total 360°.

Test 4

1. 44
2. 70
3. 10 003
4. 250 ml
5. $\frac{7}{10}$
6. 360
7. 150
8. 90
9. 70
10. 27
11. 10
12. 22:15
13. 0.9
14. 9:55
15. 5
16. 1.09
17. 12 cm
18. semi-circles
19. 49, 144, 4
20. 13:39

Notes:
- The mode is the number that occurs most often.
- Square numbers include 1, 4, 16, 25, 36, 49, 64, 81, 100, 121, 144.

Answers – Mental Maths Tests

Test 5

1. 40 016
2. 48
3. 6.7
4. 8
5. 60°
6. 104
7. 5
8. 3.7
9. 83 cm
10. 5.10 or ten past five
11. £8.50
12. 0.94
13. 1
14. 500 ml
15. 6
16. 30
17. 100
18. 1938
19. 19.2 cm
20. 27 minutes

Notes:
- A square is a special kind of rectangle with all sides equal.

Test 6

1. 390
2. 25
3. 60
4. 180°
5. 43
6. 11 cm
7. 15:50
8. −3
9. £4.88
10. 160
11. 7.15 or quarter past seven
12. 0.76
13. 6
14. 150 km
15. $\frac{3}{4}$
16. 1958
17. 24
18. 52
19. 32 × 1.7
20. 60

Notes:
- To square a number you multiply it by itself.
- Half a turn is equivalent to two right angles or 2 × 90° = total of 180°.

Test 7

1. 7
2. 30 027
3. 35
4. 80
5. 14
6. 5500 m
7. 9 or 9.0
8. 1030
9. £13.50
10. 8.25 or twenty-five past eight
11. £3.70
12. 350
13. 2
14. 250 m
15. 270°
16. 23
17. 8
18. 10
19. 40.8 cm
20. 203 ÷ 1.05

Notes:
- A prism is a shape with the same cross-section along its length, e.g. a Toblerone bar is a triangular prism.
- The edges of a 3D shape are the lines that join the corners and separate the faces.

Test 8

1. 200
2. 250
3. 17 004
4. 190 cm
5. 0.75
6. 5996
7. £1.44
8. −5°C
9. 96
10. 51
11. 48
12. 4.3
13. 4300 g
14. 7.15 a.m.
15. 7
16. 0.06
17. octagon
18. £3.50
19. 2950
20. 125°

Notes:
- The median value is the number in the middle when the set is arranged in order. If two numbers occur in the middle, the median is exactly half-way between the two numbers.

Answers – Mental Maths Tests

Test 9

1. 100
2. 35
3. 175
4. 24
5. 20:15
6. 5 cm
7. 16
8. 56
9. £3.05
10. 13
11. 3.20 or twenty past three
12. 48 cm^2
13. 9
14. 1.65
15. 0.1
16. 44
17. 2 cm
18. 1979
19. $\frac{3}{15}, \frac{5}{25}$
20. 20

Notes:
- Children often confuse area and perimeter. Perimeter is the distance all the way around the edge of a shape. The area of a shape is the amount of surface inside the shape. For rectangles, this can be calculated by multiplying the length by the breadth.

Test 10

1. 36
2. 35 days
3. 10 012
4. 8999
5. 1250 ml
6. $\frac{4}{5}$
7. £1.13
8. −1°C
9. 1.4
10. 34
11. 9
12. 16:35
13. 6.5
14. 7.30 a.m.
15. 2
16. 500
17. square
18. £2.60
19. £10.50
20. 95°

Notes:
- The modal value is the number that occurs most often.

Test 11

1. 112
2. 13 005
3. 40
4. 107
5. 46
6. 10%
7. 75 seconds
8. 28
9. 2.6
10. 89 cm
11. 11
12. 580
13. £8
14. 56 miles
15. 0 or impossible
16. 3.0999
17. 50
18. 1961
19. 70°
20. 8.2 × 5.5

Notes:
- The probability of an event that is impossible is zero.
- The angles inside a triangle have a total of 180°.

Test 12

1. 6
2. 550
3. 15:30
4. 50
5. 208 weeks
6. 360°
7. 5
8. 32
9. 74 cm
10. 150
11. 6.10 or ten past six
12. 0.93
13. 65p
14. 7.2
15. 8
16. 81
17. 27
18. 58
19. 15 cm
20. 23 minutes

National Curriculum Levels

The Key Stage 2 National Tests are levelled according to the child's total score for the written Tests A and B and one mental test, similar to those in this book.

Mark	24 or below	25–51	52–79	80–100
Level	Level 1/2	Level 3	Level 4	Level 5

Scores for each mental test can be broadly broken down as follows:

Mark	0–4	5–10	11–15	16–20
Level	Level 1/2	Level 3	Level 4	Level 5

For practice in the written tests, look for the Key Stage 2 Maths books in this series. If your child needs more practice in any Maths topics, use the WHSmith Key Stage 2 Maths Revision Guide.

Practice Pages
5-Second Questions

MORE THAN/LESS THAN

What is:

1. twelve more than twenty?
2. nineteen more than fifteen?
3. seventeen less than fifty?
4. thirty-two less than fifty?
5. four less than two thousand?
6. nine less than five hundred?

ADDING AND SUBTRACTING

Find the total of:

7. fourteen and twelve   eighteen and seventeen
8. twenty-two and nine   thirty-four and sixteen
9. Two numbers total one thousand. One of the numbers is three hundred and fifty. What is the other number?
10. Two numbers total one thousand. One of the numbers is seven hundred and twenty-five. What is the other number?

Reduce:

11. sixteen by nine
12. one hundred and ten by twenty

Decrease:

13. fifty by eleven
14. forty by six

29

Practice Pages

MULTIPLYING AND DIVIDING

What is:

15 the product of six and five?

16 the product of nine and eight?

17 five multiplied by twenty?

18 seven point two multiplied by ten?

19 twelve point nine multiplied by ten?

20 forty-two divided by six?

21 fifty-four divided by nine?

22 sixty-four divided by eight?

23 thirty-five divided by ten?

24 one hundred and sixty divided by ten?

25 Write the number that is 8 squared.

26 Write the number that is 10 squared.

27 Write the number that is 20 squared.

28 How many sides do ten pentagons have in total?

29 How many sides do seven hexagons have in total?

30 How many sides do nine octagons have in total?

Practice Pages

DOUBLING AND HALVING

31 What is **double**:

eighteen? ☐   thirty-two? ☐   fifty-six? ☐

32 What is **twice**:

thirty-nine? ☐   sixty-eight? ☐   one point six? ☐

33 What is **half**:

fifty-four? ☐   thirty-eight? ☐   eighty-eight? ☐

34 What is **half**:

sixty-two? ☐   seventy-four? ☐   ninety-six? ☐

WRITING NUMBERS IN FIGURES

Write in figures the number:

35 three thousand and two ☐

36 five thousand and nine ☐

37 eight thousand and fourteen ☐

38 nine thousand and nineteen ☐

39 ten thousand and six ☐

40 eleven thousand and eighteen ☐

41 twenty thousand and five ☐

42 thirty thousand and twenty-one ☐

43 forty thousand and thirty ☐

44 fifty thousand, four hundred ☐

Practice Pages

FRACTIONS, DECIMALS AND PERCENTAGES

What is:

45   one-third of twenty-four?

46   two-thirds of thirty?

47   one-quarter of sixty?

48   one-fifth of fifteen?

49   one-eighth of forty-eight?

50   three-quarters of twenty-four?

51   What is three-quarters as a decimal?

52   What is nine-tenths as a decimal?

53   What is six-hundredths as a decimal?

54   What is nought point two five as a fraction?

55   What is nought point three as a fraction?

56   What is nought point eight as a fraction in its simplest form?

57   Nine-tenths of the children in a class are girls.
     What percentage are girls?

58   One-fifth of the children in a class are boys.
     What percentage are boys?

59   One-quarter of the children in a class are boys.
     What percentage are boys?

Practice Pages

PROBABILITY

60 A bag contains five green cubes and one white cube. The probability of picking a green cube is five-sixths. What is the probability of picking a white cube?

61 What is the probability of a coin landing on heads? Give your answer as a fraction.

62 What is the probability that the day after July 1st will be July 2nd?

MEASUREMENT AND MONEY

How many:

63 millilitres are there in four and a half litres?

64 grams are there in five point six kilograms?

65 grams are there in three-quarters of a kilogram?

66 metres are there in one-tenth of a kilometre?

67 ten-pence coins have the same value as four pounds?

68 two-pence pieces have the same value as two pounds?

69 five-pence coins have the same value as four pounds?

70 twenty-pence pieces have the same value as ten pounds?

71 months are there in four years?

72 days are there in six weeks?

73 minutes are there in six hours?

Practice Pages

MEASUREMENT AND MONEY

74 The time is quarter to three in the afternoon. Write this time as it would be shown on a twenty-four hour digital clock.

75 The time is quarter past five in the afternoon. Write this time as it would be shown on a twenty-four hour digital clock.

76 The time is ten to nine in the evening. Write this time as it would be shown on a twenty-four hour digital clock.

77 The perimeter of a square is 24 cm. What is the length of one of its sides?

78 The perimeter of a square is 36 cm. What is the length of one of its sides?

79 The perimeter of a regular pentagon is 40 cm. What is the length of one of its sides?

80 The perimeter of a regular hexagon is 42 cm. What is the length of one of its sides?

81 How many degrees are there in a triangle?

82 How many degrees is one of the angles in an equilateral triangle?

Practice Pages
10-Second Questions

CALCULATIONS

1. Add ten and fourteen and then divide by four.
2. Multiply seven by five and then subtract seven.
3. Add fifteen and nine and then divide by three.
4. Divide two hundred by four and then subtract seven.
5. How many teams of four people can be made from a group of thirty-six people?
6. How many teams of nine people can be made from a group of fifty-four people?
7. How many teams of eight people can be made from a group of thirty-two people?
8. How many teams of four people can be made from a group of twenty-eight people?

What is:

9. three point seven multiplied by ten?
10. eleven point six multiplied by ten?
11. thirty-two point seven multiplied by one hundred?

READING SCALES

What numbers are the arrows pointing to?

12. 1000 — 2000   6.7 — 6.8

13. 800 — 1000   0.1 — 0.2

35

Practice Pages

NEGATIVE NUMBERS

14 The temperature yesterday was minus seven degrees Celsius. The temperature today is three degrees warmer. What is the temperature today?

15 The temperature yesterday was minus two degrees Celsius. The temperature today is four degrees colder. What is the temperature today?

16 The temperature yesterday was five degrees Celsius. The temperature today is seven degrees colder. What is the temperature today?

NUMBER PATTERNS AND ALGEBRA

What is the next number in the sequence?

17 58, 53, 48, 43, ☐   37, 28, 19, 10, ☐

18 1, 3, 6, 10, ☐   22, 16, 10, 4, ☐

In the equation, what is the value of *x*?

19 $x + 17 = 38$ ☐ $x - 41 = 57$ ☐

20 $33 + x = 42$ ☐ $59 - x = 21$ ☐

FRACTIONS, DECIMALS AND PERCENTAGES

21 One-quarter of a number is five. What is the number?

22 One-third of a number is twelve. What is the number?

23 One-fifth of a number is five. What is the number?

24 One-ninth of a number is four. What is the number?

25 One-sixth of a number is seven. What is the number?

26 A shop has a sale. Ten per cent is taken off all prices. What is the sale price of a book that was forty pounds?

27 In a sale, items cost twenty-five per cent of their original prices. A video costs £7 in the sale. What was its original price?

28 Circle two equivalent fractions in each row.

$\frac{1}{2}$ $\frac{2}{3}$ $\frac{3}{4}$ $\frac{1}{4}$ $\frac{2}{6}$ $\frac{6}{8}$ $\frac{7}{10}$

$\frac{1}{3}$ $\frac{5}{6}$ $\frac{6}{9}$ $\frac{2}{4}$ $\frac{5}{7}$ $\frac{1}{8}$ $\frac{2}{3}$

$\frac{1}{10}$ $\frac{2}{3}$ $\frac{9}{12}$ $\frac{1}{6}$ $\frac{2}{5}$ $\frac{4}{8}$ $\frac{3}{4}$

29 What is 10% of:

380?   490?   34?   127?

Practice Pages

MEASUREMENT AND MONEY

30 A square has sides of 4 cm. What is its perimeter?

31 A square has sides of 9 cm. What is its perimeter?

32 A regular pentagon has sides of 4 cm. What is its perimeter?

33 A regular hexagon has sides of 8 cm. What is its perimeter?

34 A square has sides of 2 cm. What is its area?

35 A square has sides of 8 cm. What is its area?

36 A rectangle has sides of 5 cm and 4 cm. What is its area?

37 What is the area of this rectangle?   3.7 cm
10 cm

38 I start with a five pound note. I spend one pound ninety-five pence. How much am I left with?

39 I start with a ten pound note. I spend three pounds seventy-five pence. How much am I left with?

40 A film started at twenty past seven. It finished at ten past eight. How many minutes did it last?

41 A film started at twenty to nine. It finished at ten o'clock. How many minutes did the film last?

Practice Pages
15-Second Questions

FRACTIONS, DECIMALS AND PERCENTAGES

1. Draw a ring around the number that is nearest to three.

   3.2   3.46   3.9   3.19   3.7

2. Draw a ring around the number that is nearest to four.

   4.11   4.46   4.089   3.8   4.39

3. Seventy-five per cent of a number is nine. What is the number?

4. Seventy-five per cent of a number is thirty-three. What is the number?

5. Thirty per cent of a number is eighteen. What is the number?

6. One-fifth of a number is twenty-five. What is the number?

CALCULATIONS OF TIME

7. A woman was born in 1897. Which birthday did she have in 1909?

8. Which year is twenty-three years before the year two thousand and two?

9. A man was born in 1887. In what year was the man's forty-ninth birthday?

Practice Pages

NUMBER KNOWLEDGE

10 Which number is exactly half-way between two thousand five hundred and three thousand?

11 Which number is exactly half-way between three thousand and six thousand?

12 Which number is exactly half-way between twenty-two and fifty-four?

13 Which number is exactly half-way between fourteen and forty-two?

MONEY PROBLEMS

14 I went to the shop with five pounds. I spent forty-five pence and then sixty-seven pence. How much did I have left?

15 I went to the shop with ten pounds. I spent eighty pence and then two pounds and fifteen pence. How much did I have left?

16 A car park costs forty pence. Twenty cars visit the car park. How much money do they pay in total?

17 A car park costs sixty pence. Eleven cars visit the car park. How much money do they pay in total?

18 I have eighty pence. My friend has three times that much. How much do we have altogether?

Practice Pages

SHAPE AND MEASUREMENT

19 What is the size of angle C?

20 What is the size of angle A?

21 What is the size of angle B?

22 How many faces does a triangular prism have?

23 How many edges does a cube have?

24 How many vertices does a square-based pyramid have?

DATA HANDLING

25 Look at the pie chart. One hundred and eighty people were asked what their favourite food was. How many people said their favourite food was chips?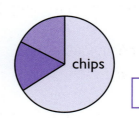

26 Here are some start and finish times of TV programmes. How long did the travel programme last?

	Start	Finish
Documentary	14:25	15:20
Travel	16:33	17:06
Wildlife	19:36	20:27

Answers
Practice Pages

5-second questions

1. 32
2. 34
3. 33
4. 18
5. 1996
6. 491

7. 26, 35
8. 31, 50
9. 650
10. 275
11. 7
12. 90
13. 39
14. 34

15. 30
16. 72
17. 100
18. 72
19. 129
20. 7
21. 6
22. 8
23. 3.5
24. 16
25. 64
26. 100
27. 400
28. 50
29. 42
30. 72

31. 36, 64, 112
32. 78, 136, 3.2
33. 27, 19, 44
34. 31, 37, 48

35. 3002
36. 5009
37. 8014
38. 9019
39. 10 006
40. 11 018
41. 20 005
42. 30 021
43. 40 030
44. 50 400

45. 8
46. 20
47. 15
48. 3
49. 6
50. 18
51. 0.75
52. 0.9
53. 0.06
54. $\frac{1}{4}$
55. $\frac{3}{10}$
56. $\frac{4}{5}$
57. 90%
58. 20%
59. 25%

60. $\frac{1}{6}$
61. $\frac{1}{2}$
62. certain or 1

63. 4500 ml
64. 5600 g
65. 750 g
66. 100 m
67. 40
68. 100
69. 80
70. 50
71. 48
72. 42
73. 360

74. 14:45
75. 17:15
76. 20:50
77. 6 cm
78. 9 cm
79. 8 cm
80. 7 cm
81. 180°
82. 60°

Answers – Practice Pages

10-second questions

1. 6
2. 28
3. 8
4. 43
5. 9
6. 6
7. 4
8. 7
9. 37
10. 116
11. 3270

12. 1300, 6.78
13. 940, 0.11

14. −4°C
15. −6°C
16. −2°C

17. 38, 1
18. 15, −2
19. 21, 98
20. 9, 38

21. 20
22. 36
23. 25
24. 36
25. 42
26. £36
27. £28
28. $\frac{3}{4}, \frac{6}{8}$
    $\frac{6}{9}, \frac{2}{3}$
    $\frac{9}{12}, \frac{3}{4}$
29. 38, 49, 3.4, 12.7

30. 16 cm
31. 36 cm
32. 20 cm
33. 48 cm
34. 4 cm^2
35. 64 cm^2
36. 20 cm^2
37. 37 cm^2
38. £3.05
39. £6.25
40. 50 minutes
41. 80 minutes

Answers – Practice Pages

15-second questions

1. 3.19
2. 4.089
3. 12
4. 44
5. 60
6. 125

7. 12th
8. 1979
9. 1936

10. 2750
11. 4500
12. 38
13. 28

14. £3.88
15. £7.05
16. £8
17. £6.60
18. £3.20

19. 105°
20. 90°
21. 95°
22. 5
23. 12
24. 5

25. 120
26. 33 minutes

Notes:
- A vertex (plural: vertices) is the mathematical word for the corner of a shape.